3 0050 05148 4714

j618.92 kah

DATE DUE

MAY 2 9 2004

DISCARD

DEMCO

D1456909

JAN   2004

DAVENPORT PUBLIC LIBRARY
321 MAIN STREET
DAVENPORT, IOWA 52801-1490

PHOBIAS

Ada P. Kahn, Ph.D. and Ronald M. Doctor, Ph.D.

Franklin Watts
A Division of Scholastic Inc.
New York • Toronto • London • Auckland • Sydney
Mexico City • New Delhi • Hong Kong
Danbury, Connecticut

Discussion of specific therapies mentioned in this book are for information only. They are not intended to provide therapy in any way and do not constitute an endorsement by the authors or publisher. Further, material in this book is not intended to provoke more anxiety in readers. Suggestions in this book are not intended as a substitute for consultation with a qualified health professional. All matters regarding your health require medical and psychological supervision. Readers are advised to consult with their personal physicians or mental—and psychological—health professionals about medical and mental-health concerns.

Cover illustration by Peter Cho.
Cover and interior design by Kathleen Santini.

Library of Congress Cataloging-in-Publication Data

Kahn, Ada P.
  Phobias / Ada P. Kahn and Ronald M. Doctor.
     p. cm. — (Life balance)
Summary: Examines what phobias are and how they differ from ordinary fears, how to cope with normal anxiety, and how to identify when and from whom to seek help.
Includes bibliographical references and index.
    ISBN 0-531-12256-5 (lib. bdg.)   0-531-15575-7 (pbk.)
    1. Phobias in children—Juvenile literature. [1. Phobias.] I. Doctor, Ronald M, (Ronald Manual) II. Title. III. Series.
    RJ506.P38K34 2003
    618.92'85225—dc21
                                        2003000034

Copyright © 2003 by Scholastic Inc.
All rights reserved. Published simultaneously in Canada.
Printed in the United States of America.
1 2 3 4 5 6 7 8 9 10 R 12 11 10 09 08 07 06 05 04 03

TABLE OF CONTENTS

One

Fear or PHOBIA?

Have you ever been afraid of a cat, a sound, or something else? If so, were the other people around you also afraid, or were you the only one who experienced the fear?

Fear is a natural reaction to a dangerous situation. The danger may be physical, leading to possible injury, such as getting hit, being attacked by an animal, falling, or seeing some unknown force coming at you out of the dark. Fear may also happen in situations where your feelings are hurt or your sense of who you are is threatened, like being made fun of, being criticized by your classmates, being picked last for a team sport, or having people angry at you.

Phobias and fears are not exactly the same. There are two differences. First, a phobia is a fearlike reaction that is out of proportion to the real danger of a situation or object. Others will not be afraid as you are. Second, a phobia will cause you to avoid this situation, person, or object in the future. For example, if one student fears snakes and has a strong reaction to seeing even a picture of a snake when others have no reaction, that is a phobia. If it is a phobia, one will also try to avoid a situation involving snakes altogether. We all share the fear of shootings in schools or of earthquakes, so those fears are not phobias—those are realistic fears.

Scared Stiff

The fear reaction usually feels like being frozen stiff, with your heart pounding, finding it hard to breathe, sweating, being very alert, and often trembling. These are unpleasant reactions that many young people experience when they are afraid—and when they are facing things, people, or situations where fear or anxiety arises. The terms "fear" and "anxiety" are close in meaning, but "phobia" refers to fears that disrupt daily, regular activities and interfere with everyday life.

Fear comes when there is danger and leaves when the danger has passed. However, fear also gets attached to the general situation and becomes conditioned to that situation, or even to thoughts of the feared situation. Let's say you go to the dentist and feel some pain. The next time your parents say you have to go to the dentist, you'll probably experience some feelings of fear even though you are not yet in the dentist's chair or near the office. Just the word "dentist" creates fear for you, as do images of the dentist and dental instruments.

Running for Your Life

Human beings must have certain things in order to live, such as oxygen, food, water, a place to live, and safety from anything that threatens to harm us. Things that threaten us often lead to fearful withdrawal or avoidance of these things. Think about how small land animals run away from fire or get out of water into which they have fallen. Researchers say that abrupt, loud noises frighten most people and animals. Fear serves as a way to activate or arouse people so they can protect themselves or run away from danger. It has helped humans survive.

People learn fear reactions by attaching fears to people, things, or situations that are present when they have the original strong reaction. The fear reaction spreads over to many things associated with the dentist and with the pain you experienced in the dentist's office. You can even learn fear by watching people who are afraid in a movie or just by seeing people, such as friends, hurt or injured.

Fear becomes a phobia when we start to avoid the people, situations, things, or even words that produce our individual or uncommon fear reaction. Let's say you start avoiding going to the dentist. Maybe you claim to be sick or have a headache or stomachache before the trip and plead with your parents not to go. You are avoiding a situation that you associate with physical pain and fear. Phobias can produce many feelings in the body and mind,

Fear becomes a phobia when we start to avoid the people, situations, things, or even words that produce our individual or uncommon fear reaction.

such as stomachaches, body pains, worries, doubts, anger, headaches, an inability to sleep, and other symptoms.

What Causes Fears?

As human beings, we inherit some specific fears. It is normal to have these fears because all of us have them to some degree. These include being separated from parents or caregivers, being attacked by animals, looking down over an edge from high places, being confronted by angry people or strangers, or being watched while performing. These fears have helped humans survive throughout history, and everyone has them to some degree. Other fears can develop in different ways:

- Some fears are learned because of examples set by parents or other adults. When Kaitlin was a little girl, her mother always said, "Let's not cross the street. There is a dog over there." Kaitlin learned to be afraid of dogs by observing her mother's avoidance of dogs.
- A natural disaster—such as a fire, flood, or tornado— or an airplane or train crash, can also produce fears. The more intense the memory and the desire to avoid a repeat situation, the more intense the fear will be.
- Some fears happen for no obvious reason. Many of these go away over time, as people get older and have new experiences.

Common Phobias and Fears

Psychologists have found that some fears tend to develop at certain ages as children are growing up, and then gradually disappear in the teenage years. Others start in the teen years and last into adulthood. Many young people are afraid of doctors and dentists and may have had painful experiences with them.

IDENTIFYING YOUR PERSONAL FEARS

You may wonder what kind of fears you have and how strong they are. If you have these questions, take some time to complete this questionnaire, which describes various areas of young people's fears. This is not a diagnostic test; it is meant only to give you an idea of the kinds of fears you have and how strong they are. If the fears are intense, it is important for you to seek help and support from your parents and possibly a professional.

For each item below, select a number from 1 to 10 that reflects how intense your reaction is and how much you try to avoid these situations. Write the number in the box opposite each common fear situation.

 0 = no noticeable reaction

1–3 = slight reaction but no avoidance

4–6 = noticeable reaction; want to avoid but can stay if necessary

7–9 = very uncomfortable with many physical reactions; definitely want to avoid

 10 = really scared and unable to think clearly or to perform; always avoid

FEAR SITUATION	NUMBER
Traveling (bus, train, car, or airplane)	
Being left alone for a long time	
Being where other people will look at you (elevators, open spaces, and sitting in the center of a row of seats)	

FEAR SITUATION	NUMBER
Experiencing the death of a parent	
Receiving an injection or seeing blood or injuries	
Going to a hospital or undergoing a medical or dental procedure	
Being faced with small animals or insects	
Being around angry people or hearing sudden loud noises	
Being in closed-in spaces	
Being watched or stared at	
Talking to people in authority	
Being criticized	
Speaking to your class or a group of classmates	
Getting bad grades	
Being in a terrorist attack	
Other situations specific to you (fluttering birds, taking elevators, etc.)	
Total score	

IDENTIFYING YOUR PERSONAL FEARS
(CONTINUED)

What can you learn from your answers? First, notice the types of items you scored high and low on. Do the items where you scored high fit together? For example, many items have to do with other people's possible reactions to you. Did you score high on these social items? Other groups of items have to do with being hurt or injured, another with being alone. Some have to do with criticism and failure, while others involve animals.

Your total score on this scale can also be meaningful. In general, your score can be divided into one of three broad ranges. If your score is 60 to 90, you are somewhat fearful, perhaps about specific things, situations, or people, but your reaction is not intense. If your total score is between 90 and 110, you are moderately fearful and probably will benefit from the ideas presented in this book. Finally, if your score is above 110, your reaction is strong enough that you should talk with your parents about it. See Chapter 5 to find out more about how to seek assistance and who to go to for help.

The most common fears in childhood are of animals and snakes. They usually begin between the ages of two and four and usually go away by age ten, unless some traumatic experience with an animal or snake makes the fear become a phobia. The most common fear from ages ten to thirteen is that of the darkness or what might be lurking in the darkness. Thunder and lightning are also common fears but usually go away by the teenage years. Very young children often are afraid of strangers, but this also usually goes away with age. Almost all children are afraid of being left alone for long periods of time (until the teenage years when they like being with friends). Most are afraid of their parents dying, and this fear usually intensifies until young adulthood.

By adolescence, most children outgrow many of their fears. Only two fears get stronger in adolescence: fear of being looked at and fear of blushing. These fears occur earlier in girls than in boys and are related to the effect people can have or the effect of being with people. (See Chapter 3, Social Phobias, where these reactions will be covered in more detail.)

Many phobias begin with a traumatic experience, such as a terrible car accident, a medical operation, a near drowning, or the death of a relative, classmate, or pet.

There can be many other types of phobias, but they occur less frequently. Many of these other phobias begin with a traumatic experience, such as a terrible car accident,

Common Fears by Age				
Fear	Age			
	10	11	12	13
Death of a parent	X			
Parents' divorce	X	X		
Personal danger	X	X		
Kidnapping; burglary	X			
The dark	X			
War, terrorism	X	X	X	X
Plane or car crashes			X	X
Medical procedures	X	X	X	
Injections	X	X	X	
Drug use			X	X
Heights	X	X	X	X
Strangers	X	X	X	
Animals	X	X	X	
New situations	X	X		

a medical operation (receiving anesthesia), a near drowning, or the death of a relative, classmate, or pet.

Finally, young people of all ages can develop school phobia. This is a strong desire to avoid school because of fears of something happening at school or in the classroom, or of being separated from parents. School phobia requires help not only for the child but also the parents, who may be supporting the avoidance behavior even though they are unaware that they are doing so.

Listed below are common adult fears, which may also develop in children. Remember, if the situation, thing, or person causes avoidance, the condition is called a phobia.

- public speaking
- making mistakes
- failure
- taking tests
- angry people
- being alone
- blood and injury
- injections
- dentists
- rejection
- disapproval
- authority figures
- flying in airplanes

Phobias have long names. Here are a few:

Phobia	Name
Fear of the dark	Nyctophobia
Fear of heights	Acrophobia
Fear of birds	Ornithophobia
Fear of fish	Ichthyophobia
Fear of cats	Ailurophobia or gatophobia
Fear of change or new things	Neophobia
Fear of mirrors	Eisoptrophobia
Fear of reptiles, snakes	Herpetophobia, ophidiophobia

Anxiety Disorders

Phobias are a type of anxiety disorder. Anxiety is a feeling of uneasiness about something happening in the future. It is a combination of nervousness (like fear) and worrying (the anticipation of fear). Of course, we all get a little nervous and worried at times, but when carried to an extreme, the situation becomes an anxiety disorder.

There are many different types of anxiety disorders, such as phobias (including social phobia), panic attacks, post-traumatic stress disorder, and obsessive-compulsive disorder. Without treatment, these disorders can take over a person's life. However, there are effective treatments for anxiety disorders that can help control the symptoms.

Social Phobia

One of the most common kinds of anxiety disorder is social phobia. Social worries are common in young people. Most of us want to look our best, be liked by others, and fit in, but it's not always as easy as it seems. Twelve-year-old Ashley had always been big for her age, but it never bothered her until recently. Lately, she felt as if she just didn't fit in with her classmates. "Most kids think I'm older than twelve. But I don't fit in with the older kids because they can do a lot more things than I can, and I don't fit in with kids my age because they haven't grown yet."

Some young people find that being with others makes them extremely nervous and fearful. Some may avoid situations out of fear of being criticized, being looked at, or not wanting to make mistakes. When avoidance becomes a pattern, it is called social phobia. Most young people grow out of social fears as they learn to relate better to others, learn how to take criticism, and feel more self-confident.

Some common examples of social fears are:

- worrying about how you look
- fearing criticism from your friends or from adults
- worrying about failing in school or in sports
- avoiding situations where people will be watching you talk, perform, or participate in sports

Ashley found a good way to adapt to her uncomfortable feelings and fears of not being accepted. She tried out for the soccer team, and discovered that she was good at sports. Now, her teammates are her best friends, and other kids admire her on the field. "I feel good about myself," says Ashley.

Panic Attacks

A panic attack is an intense feeling of sudden and overwhelming fear, making it hard to think or take action. It is literally being scared stiff. A person who is having a panic attack can't move or make a good decision. However, panic attacks are not very common in young people.

When people have panic attacks, they feel they must relieve their feelings of intense fear or terror as quickly as possible, often by getting away from the situation. Feelings during a panic attack may include numbness and tingling in the legs and feeling sweaty or faint. The heart beats fast, and it becomes hard to breathe. In fact, these symptoms are so severe that many adults who experience a panic attack think they are having a heart attack.

Agoraphobia

Agoraphobia refers to a disabling group of phobias that usually do not affect young children but may begin in the teenage years. Agoraphobia involves avoidance of public places, such as crowded malls and streets, public transportation, and enclosed places (for example, elevators and tunnels). It also involves a fear of being far away from a safe place or being far from help. Sometimes it begins with a panic attack, and the person becomes fearful that another attack will happen. Agoraphobia also involves a fear of losing control of or embarrassing oneself.

Post-Traumatic Stress Disorder

When the house next door to Zach was broken into one night, it was natural for him to be scared. "I heard the glass patio door breaking. Then I heard shouts, and my Dad ran outside to chase the burglar." The police arrived in time to catch the intruder, but that didn't put an end to Zach's fears. "Even though my Dad came back OK, now I can't sleep at night. It's been two months since then, and I lie in bed worrying that a burglar will get into our house and hurt someone in my family."

Such a terrifying episode could be considered a trauma—a physical or emotional injury that has a lasting effect. People who experience trauma may begin to develop unusual and uncomfortable symptoms, such as Zach's inability to fall asleep. Those feelings and symptoms often continue long after the episode itself has ended. When these feelings and symptoms persist, the situation is known as post-traumatic stress disorder (PTSD). Some common aftereffects of trauma and symptoms of post-traumatic stress disorder include:

- bad dreams
- inability to sleep
- extreme nervousness and anxiety when you see or hear something that reminds you of the earlier incident (accident, shooting, burglary)
- similar discomforts in your body—such as sweating, nausea, or butterflies in the stomach—that you had at the time of the trauma when something reminds you of it or when you just think about it

For Zach, his lack of sleep began to affect his schoolwork. His teacher noticed his sleepiness during the day and called in his parents. When Zach explained why he couldn't sleep, his parents tried to reassure him. They showed him that the double locks on their front and back doors couldn't be opened from the outside. They also installed a motion-sensitive device near their front and back doors so bright lights would turn on if anyone came near during the night. With this understanding, Zach began to sleep at night and do better in school.

Responding to Disaster

According to the National Mental Health Association (NMHA), young people have little experience to help them place their current situation into perspective. That is why children respond differently to disasters, depending on their understanding, background, and maturity, says the NMHA. A terrible event can create worry in young people because they may interpret the disaster as a personal danger to themselves and those they care about.

According to the Federal Emergency Management Agency, after a disaster, children are the ones most afraid that the event will happen again, that someone will be injured or killed, that they will be separated from their family, and that they will be left alone. With help from parents or caregivers and guidance from counselors, young people can allay their worries and come to understand that some of these fears are exaggerated or unrealistic.

Like Zach, confiding in your parents is a good first step in facing your fears. With an understanding of exactly what your fears are, when they happen, and how you feel, your parents—as well as health professionals—can help you overcome them. Remember, trauma can stay with you the rest of your life, so be sure to ask for help as soon as you need it.

Obsessive-Compulsive Disorder (OCD)

In severe cases, phobias can alter our behavior to the point of being disruptive. You may have developed certain patterns of behavior because you think they will help reduce anxiety. For example, as you get ready for school, you may check and recheck everything in your backpack so many

OCD Starts Early

According to Isaac Marks, M.D., author of Fears, Phobias and Rituals, *while obsessive-compulsive disorder is not very common in children, many obsessive-compulsive adults say their problem started before they were fifteen years old and came on gradually. In some cases, the child may not even be aware when it starts. Researchers report that nearly all affected children involve their parents and sometimes siblings in their rituals. For example, they might make repeated requests for reassurance, demand daily cooperation in rituals, and dominate practically every action in the home, with shouting and violent tempers if family members hesitate to obey.*

times that you miss your bus in the morning. Or, before going to bed at night, you make sure that all your books are perfectly arranged on the shelf, repositioning them over and over again. You might be using these rituals to reduce anxieties brought on by fearful thoughts. You may fear that something bad will happen if you don't repeat these rituals.

A compulsion is an intense feeling that one must perform certain acts, or behaviors, such as rituals. Rituals lower anxiety, and so they tend to be repeated. Rituals such as handwashing or keeping things in order are common.

An obsession is an unwanted recurrent and persistent thought or image. It causes anxiety and feelings of discomfort. These intense feelings cause one to believe that if a certain act is not performed over and over again, something terrible will happen. When obsessions and compulsions occur, it is known as obsessive-compulsive disorder or OCD. OCD can be overcome with professional help. Some common symptoms of OCD are:

- feeling that you must perform certain acts (rituals) over and over
- being aware that worrisome thoughts are not wanted and not realistic

OCD is very uncommon in young people. However, many people who develop anxieties begin expressing them at a young age, so it is important to understand OCD.

Two

Feeling AFRAID

Think about how you felt the last time you were afraid of something. Did you get a stomachache? Did you feel out of breath? Fear can cause unpleasant sensations or feelings in your body as well as in your mind. You may feel sick to your stomach, sweat a lot, notice a faster heartbeat, be out of breath, and feel that your muscles are tense. These feelings are sometimes accompanied by constant worry or bad dreams.

These feelings in both your body and mind may actually start before you are aware that you are afraid of something. For many young people, worry sometimes begins to set in even before they notice

HOW DO WE RESPOND TO FEAR?

For many young people, responses to fear seem to be felt most in body sensations such as shortness of breath, a strong heartbeat, and sweating. Others experience fear in their thoughts or in having strong emotional reactions such as trembling or being unable to move. To help you understand your own responses to fearful situations, complete this questionnaire while imagining yourself in a fearful situation. Remember, it is not a diagnostic evaluation; you would need an expert for that. It will only help you to understand more about your fears. You may want to ask your parents to work with you on this. This questionnaire will help you know more about your:

- Body sensations
- Thought reactions
- Behavioral reactions

In the following chart, rate yourself after each item with: always (2 points), sometimes (1 point), and never (0 points). Then add up all the numbers in each of the three sections. If you score 14 or more in any one category, you may want to consider talking about your fears with parents or a professional.

BODY SENSATIONS	POINTS
My stomach flutters or feels full (butterflies).	
I feel nauseated.	
I sweat or feel cold.	
My heart beats fast.	
My face gets hot.	

BODY SENSATIONS	POINTS
I have to go to the toilet often.	
My mouth becomes dry.	
I get a headache.	
It's hard to breathe.	
Subtotal score:	

THOUGHT REACTIONS	POINTS
I think about losing control.	
I worry about horrible things happening to me.	
I can't think clearly.	
Angry thoughts come to me.	
Jealous thoughts come to me.	
I dwell on situations, thinking about them over and over.	
I have trouble concentrating.	
I have nightmares.	
At times, my thoughts seem to be strange and unwanted.	
Subtotal score:	

BEHAVIORAL REACTIONS	POINTS
I stutter or stammer.	
I clench my teeth and grind them.	

HOW DO WE RESPOND TO FEAR?
(CONTINUED)

BEHAVIORAL REACTIONS	POINTS
I bite my nails.	
I pick at things (hair, lint, etc.).	
I check things over and over again.	
I want to keep on eating all the time.	
I have to be active all the time (fidget and wring my hands).	
I have trouble sleeping.	
I cry a lot.	
Subtotal score:	
Total score: **(Add the three subtotal scores together)**	

From this test, you can be more aware of what your responses to fear really are. See if you can tell whether your main reactions are sensations in your body, thought reactions, or behavioral reactions. Your highest score is where your fear reaction starts first and where it is probably the strongest.

There are specific kinds of relaxation exercises for each area that will help you cope with these reactions. Breathing helps reduce body sensations, meditation helps to slow thoughts, and progressive relaxation helps with behavioral reactions. You'll read about these relaxation exercises later.

they are afraid. Worrying and anxiety often relate to future events, such as going to school and being picked on by a bully, having to give a report in front of the class, not being chosen for the class play, or seeing certain animals on the street.

Worry means being fearful of the future and thinking about what could happen. It is saying "What if...?" You probably think of the worst possible thing that might happen. This can make you feel anxious and uncomfortable.

Jonathan, age twelve, has a phobia about snakes. He began worrying about his upcoming class trip to the zoo a month ahead of time. "Just thinking about the snakes gets me scared. What if the snakes get out of the cage? I think about that so much I can't even do my homework."

Coping Skills

Coping skills are practical solutions that people use to deal with everyday challenges as well as disturbing situations. Examples include how you face taking a test, getting ready for a trip, or reacting when a parent is ill or someone you love dies. Coping skills enable people to make use of their past experiences in difficult situations. Such skills make people able to meet new situations head on with confidence and flexibility. Deep breathing and imagination techniques are forms of coping skills one can learn to help overcome reactions to fearful situations.

Jonathan got headaches and had trouble thinking straight every time the idea of a snake came into his head. He had unpleasant reactions in both his body and his mind.

Ready...Set...What's Your Trigger?

Fear usually has a trigger or something that sets it off. The fear trigger can be anything from a sight, smell, or sound to a thought that reminds you of a fearful situation. For example, Natasha's soccer coach was killed by a bolt of lightning on the school soccer field. Now whenever she hears a loud noise that sounds like thunder, she gets scared and worried. "I feel like I might throw up. It's really uncomfortable," says Natasha, who is eleven years old.

Matthew begins feeling afraid just by thinking about riding on the school bus and possibly getting hit again by a bully. "I made excuses not to go to school. My stomach hurt. My head hurt. Every morning I nearly threw up. My mother believed me at first. Then she got suspicious, and I had to tell her the truth. There was a bully, an older kid, on the school bus and I was so afraid he would hit me again."

Fear triggers are situations, things, or people that make you start to feel afraid. Examples of some common fear triggers are:
- hearing thunder
- thinking about the bully on the school bus

- smelling smoke or fire
- thinking about performing or speaking in front of the class

Fear triggers are situations, things, or people that make you start to feel afraid.

You may be aware of some of the triggers that start your feelings of fearfulness. Sit down and make a list of the ones you know about. Go through your list of body sensations, thought reactions, and behavioral reactions to help remind you of your various types of fears and reactions. Then you can start to think about what sets them off. Emotions themselves can be triggers. Many young people get angry or jealous. These feelings can trigger anxiety.

There are probably some triggers that you do not know about. To find out what they are, start keeping a diary. Write down the following things when you are aware of fearful feelings:

- the date, day, and time of your fearful episode
- what is going on around you at the time (triggers)
- how your body feels (for example, stomachache)
- what you are worrying about (thoughts)

Then, after a week or more, review your diary and try to find patterns. You may want to ask your parents to help you review your diary.

What Is the Circle of Fear?

For many young people like Jonathan, Natasha, and Matthew, there is a circle of fear. According to David Clark, an Oxford University psychologist, as people become aware of sensations in their bodies, they begin to worry and become anxious, which makes the bodily sensations get worse. Soon they become afraid of those sensations, and they start to

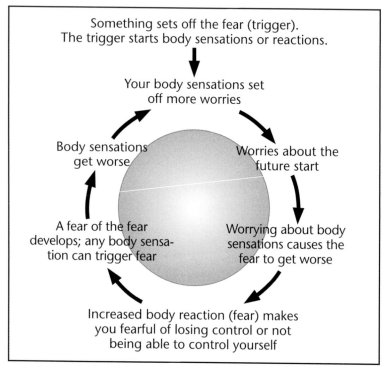

Something sets off the fear (trigger).
The trigger starts body sensations or reactions.

Your body sensations set off more worries

Body sensations get worse

Worries about the future start

A fear of the fear develops; any body sensation can trigger fear

Worrying about body sensations causes the fear to get worse

Increased body reaction (fear) makes you fearful of losing control or not being able to control yourself

The circle of fear is a fear of the body sensations associated with the fear reaction. Then the body sensations themselves trigger the fear reaction.

avoid the situation, thing, or person. If they avoid the situation, they become less anxious, but in the long run, their avoidance makes the circle of fear stronger and more difficult to deal with. For example, Jonathan's avoidance of school because of the zoo field trip makes his fear of snakes worse and soon he might fear even riding past the zoo on a bus.

When you understand what your sensations are, you can start to overcome them and reduce your fear reactions. For example, if you scored high on the body sensations section, practicing slow breathing with long exhalations will help you relax.

If your thought reactions score was high, learning to listen to your good or rational thoughts will help control your fears. A high thought reactions score means that you are telling yourself scary thoughts and will need to work on changing them. Look to see what you are telling yourself that makes a situation so scary. This is the catastrophic thought that you are adding to the situation—the part you need to let go of. Imagine the situation without this added-on scary part. Calmly picture yourself going to the dentist, being in the chair, and letting go of the thought of pain and injury.

If your behavioral reactions score is high, then you need to learn how to work through your emotions. Don't let fears disrupt your life and interfere with what you want to do. Avoidance may feel good at the time, but it does not solve the problem.

Three
Social
PHOBIAS

O f all phobias—among young people as well as adults—social phobias are the most common. Social phobias are really fears of being with people. Because many social phobias begin when people are still young, it is important to understand them and learn to overcome them as early as possible. Having a social phobia in later life can interfere with personal and family life, school, and work.

When is a worry about social occasions just a worry or anxiety and when is it a phobia? How can you tell the difference? Most people want to be liked or accepted, and to avoid criticism. Some thoughts that do *not* represent phobias but that are part of everyday life are: Am I wearing the right clothes to the party? Will I look funny eating? Can I talk in front of the class without stammering? What if I forget my lines in the play? What if I start sweating at the party? Will they notice if I blush? Will my hand shake when I write on the blackboard? What will I talk about at the party?

These worries, or social anxieties, include a wide range of feelings. When the feelings are carried to an extreme, so that one avoids the situation (not just thinking or worrying about it), the situation may be called social phobia or social anxiety disorder.

Some of the most common social phobias are:
- fear of being looked at by others (perhaps while standing in front of the class)
- fear of blushing in front of others
- fear of being touched or standing close to others
- fear of being teased or criticized
- fear of failure
- fear of looking bad to others
- fear of strangers
- fear of urinating or defecating in public rest rooms
- fear of eating with others watching

Shyness or Social Phobia?

Almost everyone experiences shyness at some time, especially in certain situations, such as meeting new boys or girls or a new teacher for the first time. Extreme shyness is a symptom of social anxiety and is related to a fear of being looked at unfavorably by others. It may also be related to low self-esteem.

How can you tell if you are shy? Physically, shy people may blush and perspire. Emotionally, they may feel anxious and insecure. Shy people may think that no one wants to talk to them or that no one likes them.

In fact, a shy person's behavior may actually discourage getting to know new people because shy people tend to keep their heads down and even avoid eye contact with others. Shyness may bring on a lack of social relationships and cause the shy person to feel lonely.

In fact, a shy person's behavior may actually discourage getting to know new people because shy people tend to keep their heads down and even avoid eye contact with others.

People deal with shyness in several ways, depending on their own style of handling situations. Some people withdraw and become quiet in social situations, while others force themselves to cover up their shyness by trying to be the life of the party. In fact, some shy people have actually become performers or public figures, handling their shyness by keeping themselves in controlled situations, performing well-rehearsed roles in familiar situations.

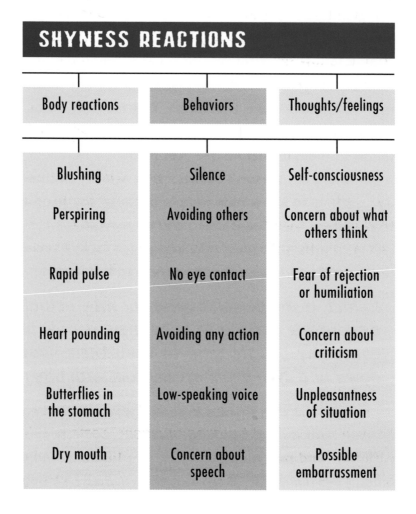

SHYNESS REACTIONS

Body reactions	Behaviors	Thoughts/feelings
Blushing	Silence	Self-consciousness
Perspiring	Avoiding others	Concern about what others think
Rapid pulse	No eye contact	Fear of rejection or humiliation
Heart pounding	Avoiding any action	Concern about criticism
Butterflies in the stomach	Low-speaking voice	Unpleasantness of situation
Dry mouth	Concern about speech	Possible embarrassment

How Do Social Phobias Start?

Some social phobias may develop over many months while others develop over several years. Some may be brought on by a specific event, such as being neglected at a party, or having said the wrong thing to a friend's parent. About half the people who have social phobias are shy and always have been. Some had unpleasant things happen to them, such as being ridiculed, criticized, or humiliated in front of others when they were young.

How parents behave may influence some young people's social phobias. For example, parents who have few friends and are socially anxious in front of others may influence their children to react in similar ways. Unlike some phobias, which tend to go away as one grows older, social phobias persist and are equally common among girls and boys.

Stage Fright

Stage fright is probably the most common form of social phobia. It is a persistent fear of exposure to criticism in certain situations, particularly in public speaking or in dramatic, musical, or other types of performances. This is a type of extreme fear that affects people as they are being watched, such as while making a speech, playing a musical instrument, or performing in a chorus or a play. People who have stage fright and a phobia about being in front of others will avoid these situations.

Stage fright is related to a fear of making a mistake in front of others or of looking foolish. A variation of stage fright involves a fear of others seeing you shaking while you write something on a blackboard and also a fear of others seeing you urinating. Some stress and nervousness is natural and may even make your performance better because stress pumps more energy into the body, making you more alert and motivated. However, when the pressure becomes extreme, the effects on physical and emotional well being can be destructive and you will go out of your way to avoid performance situations.

Some stress and nervousness is natural and may even make your performance better because stress pumps more energy into the body, making you more alert and motivated.

Stage fright prompts certain feelings in your body, thoughts, and emotions. You may have a dry mouth, a lump in your throat, a rapid heartbeat, trembling, sweating, an upset stomach, frequent urination, and a feeling of being "frozen stiff." Other reactions are headaches, skin and stomach problems, and hot and cold flashes. As these feelings get stronger, one may become increasingly involved with overcoming them, which takes away energy to think, concentrate, and be creative. These strong feelings can become a phobia, and the phobic person may then avoid any performance situation that might provoke fears. However, many people learn to overcome these feelings and go through with their performance—even though they experience strong negative feelings before each performance.

The Look of Stage Fright

How does a person who has stage fright look?

- *voice quivers or stammers*
- *perspires*
- *paces, sways, shuffles feet, knees tremble*
- *has distracting arm and hand movements (fidgets, scratches, wrings hands, keeps hands in pockets)*
- *hands shake*
- *avoids eye contact*
- *face muscles are tense, the face is pale or flushed*
- *moistens lips often, clears throat often*

Self-Esteem and Social Phobias

If you feel good about yourself and like yourself just as you are, you have a healthy self-esteem. However, if your self-esteem is low, you are more likely to become anxious in social situations and even get to the point of avoiding others. People who are shy and low in self-esteem are more likely than others to develop social phobias.

How can you improve your self-esteem? First, think about your good qualities. What do you like about yourself? Do you excel in a sport? Are you a quick learner? Are your grades good? Second, tell yourself positive statements, such as, "I will look as good as the others at that party." "My clothes will be just right." "I will have interesting things to say when I meet my friend's parents." Saying is believing. Say these things, called positive affirmations, over to yourself and soon you will believe them. Remember, you are your worst critic. What you say about yourself is far worse than what others say about you.

Finally, talk with your parents about your self-esteem concerns. You may fear that you will be criticized for some aspects of your personality, appearance, or behavior. Parents or other family members can be helpful in reassuring you that how you look or what you might

What you say about yourself is far worse than what others say about you.

say will be just right. They know you best. They can give you honest reactions and help you see the best side of yourself and, if necessary, get help for you to overcome your fears about social situations.

Four

Overcoming Your PHOBIAS

nce you have a better understanding of what your phobia is and how you react, the next step is to learn how to overcome that phobia. Overcoming your phobia will take some time; changes are usually slow to happen. Work at your own pace, and don't be discouraged if you take one step forward and then feel like you have fallen back. Young people who have succeeded in overcoming phobias say that sometimes they have to repeat a step again and again before moving ahead. So, be patient.

You have already learned how to identify your phobias. Do you want to change a particular reaction with the situation, thing, or person? What will happen if you are less fearful in this situation or with this thing or person? It is good to think about how it would be to feel better. This will motivate you to work on overcoming your phobia. See where your strongest reactions were on the body sensations, thought reactions, and behavioral reactions categories in Chapter 2.

When you have this understanding, figure out what triggers (sets off) your fearful reactions. Think about how and when the fears and fear reactions begin. Under what conditions? Also see where it does *not* occur and where you feel safe in the situation or with the thing or person. Then, start planning your own personal way to gradually face and cope with your phobias.

Let's say that you are fearful of new situations, particularly of going to parties where you don't know many people. Many things may go through your mind, such as thoughts that no one will talk with you or that others won't like you. You may also worry that they may be critical of how you look or act. You may avoid these situations altogether if you are fearful and have a social phobia.

Approach rather than avoid social situations. However, take very small steps so intense fear or anxiety does not occur. First, look at the social situations you have identified as worrisome or fear provoking. Ask yourself this question: "What catastrophic or horrible idea am I adding to the situation that makes it so bad?" Some examples of catastrophic thoughts might be:

- No one will like me and I will be all alone.
- Everyone might laugh at me (or not laugh with me).
- No one is interested in me.

Now, notice that what makes this situation so bad is the unrealistic expectation. It is not that someone could laugh at you, it's that *everyone* will laugh at you. The concept of "everyone" is something you have added that makes the situation so scary. Or, you could make a demand that is unrealistic such as "everyone has to like me." It would be nice if everyone liked you but that is unrealistic. So, take a look at what negative or catastrophic thought you add to the situation that makes it more difficult. You will have to change and let go of this thought in order to be comfortable. There are two ways to begin to change these kinds of thoughts:

- Catch yourself saying or thinking the catastrophic idea (demand or unrealistic expectation) and stop it. Use a rubber band to stop it or just say "Stop." (This is what is known as thought-stopping.) Then, notice that there are some uncomfortable parts of the situation but that they are not catastrophic.

- Relax and imagine yourself being in the situation (even though there are some uncomfortable parts). Don't let the catastrophic part in. Let go of the bad, unrealistic thoughts or demands. See if you can imagine the situation for up to two minutes without intrusive catastrophic thoughts.

Think about how and when your fearful feelings start. You may recall situations at parties when you felt uncomfortable. Maybe people seemed to be looking at you or you said something and they didn't respond or, worse, even laughed. These are triggers. Think about what was happening before the fear started. "I said no to a lot of parties," says twelve-year-old David. "I never knew what to talk about. I always stood aside when groups of kids talked and joked and I felt left out. My parents noticed that as soon as an invitation came I would get withdrawn and quiet. The mail was the trigger for my phobia and stomachaches. My bad feelings got worse until I called to say I wasn't coming."

"As soon as an invitation came I would get withdrawn and quiet...My bad feelings got worse until I called to say I wasn't coming."

2. Practice picturing this until you can see it in your mind and feel comfortable. Next, imagine that five of the six people respond but one does not (for whatever reason). Picture this while breathing deeply until you feel comfortable.

3. Now imagine that two people do not respond. Practice until you are comfortable with this mental image.

4. Imagine talking with old friends and meeting new friends at the party. Imagine eating foods you like. Imagine yourself having a good time. Realize that you can be in the situation and feel okay. Do this imagination exercise several times over a period of days before you answer the invitation.

5. Finally, since you can imagine being in a group and not minding that not all the people respond to you, it is time to practice in a real situation. Take it slow, and breathe. Also, think ahead about what to say in the real situation, maybe telling someone that you like his shirt or responding to what people are saying.

Before going to the party, David used this imagination technique and thought about some interesting stories to tell his friends. He thought about video games he had played recently. Those ideas helped him get a conversation going. In the end, he felt comfortable in the situation and good about himself.

BREATHING EASY

Most of the time breathing is natural and easy. In stressful situations, however, you may sometimes hold your breath or take short, uneven breaths without realizing it. This often makes the feelings in your body and mind even worse.

Breathing in is called *respiration*. Breathing out is called *ventilation*. Respiration puts oxygen into body cells, and ventilation removes excess carbon dioxide. Holding your breath, as well as taking shallow irregular breaths, can bring on stressful feelings.

Deep breathing with a lung exhalation is the basis for many relaxation techniques. You can change the circle of anxiety and fear by controlling your breath. Deep breathing from your diaphragm (your middle) helps you relax. As soon as you are aware of your trigger of fear, think about breathing and try to control the fear by taking deep, slow breaths. Posture can also affect breathing. Stand or sit straight, keep your body in alignment, and you will have more lung capacity to breathe better.

Many behavior therapies include control of breathing. Try the technique below to start thinking about breathing in a whole new way. By doing this type of breathing when you think about a fearful situation, you can help yourself relax and overcome the bodily sensations caused by fear. Ask a parent or friend to work with you as you learn this technique.

- Lie comfortably on your back on a padded floor or a firm bed.

Close your eyes. Keep your arms at your sides, not touching your body, with your palms up.

- Keep your legs straight out and slightly apart with your toes pointed comfortably outward. Use pillows under your knees and under your head to make you more comfortable.

- Focus attention on your breathing. Breathe in through your nose. Breathe out through your mouth. Place your hand on the area of your abdomen that seems to rise and fall the most as you inhale (breathe in) and exhale (breathe out).

- Place both hands lightly on your abdomen just below your navel and slow your breathing. Become aware of how your abdomen rises with each inhalation and falls with each exhalation. Breathe out through your mouth. Count to three as you breathe in, hold it for two counts, and then let it out to a count of six. (That's a rhythm of 3–2–6.) Exhale completely. If you have difficulty breathing into your abdomen, press your hand gently down on your abdomen as you breathe out and let your abdomen push your hand back up as you breathe in.

Observe how your chest moves. It should be moving at the same rate as your abdomen. Practice this 3–2–6 rhythm of breathing each day until you begin to feel relaxation regularly while breathing. Eventually you will be able to do this breathing technique without lying down. Try this technique as you think about your fear triggers, then practice and imagine facing the scary things while being relaxed.

Buddy Backup

While changing your reactions to fear is really an individual matter up to you, you may find it helpful to have a friend who understands and is willing to help you. For example, when you decide that you'd really like to go to a party, have imagined yourself in the situation, and have overcome some of the feelings of fear in your body and mind, enlist the help of a friend. Go to the party together, and stay together until you feel comfortable mingling with others. Then get back together from time to time to compare notes and perhaps introduce each other to new people.

Go to the party together, and stay together until you feel comfortable mingling with others.

The first time you go to a party, you may feel comfortable for a while and then some fearful feelings might come up. You might want to back away from any triggers (such as crowds of people) and talk with your friend. Use your new breathing technique, and let the fear reaction calm down. Then, when you feel ready, go back to the party. If you can't bring your fear reaction down by backing off, then leave the party with your friend—there will be lots of other opportunities.

You may use the technique of backing off once or twice. Having your friend around will give you strength. The next time you go to a party, as you feel more comfortable, you will want to stay and enjoy the whole event, with or without someone else.

With less fear of social situations, you will feel confident about yourself and your social skills will get better and better. In fact, you may even get excited about receiving party invitations. Remember, you don't have to be the most popular person there—just have a good time!

Getting **HELP**

Five

Phobias can produce unwanted and intense emotions. For example, some young people have a phobia of taking tests. They may develop physical symptoms just thinking about the test. Others are afraid of standing up in front of their class to speak. Still others may have specific phobias about riding in elevators, crossing bridges, going to doctors, getting injections, or seeing certain types of animals. They may experience depression, jealousy, difficulty sleeping, concentration problems, social anxieties, or a negative view of themselves. Some people go out of their way to avoid fearful situations but wish they did not. Regardless of the reason for wanting to have counseling, the basic factor is wanting to feel better about themselves.

Usually it takes time to reduce reactions to your phobias. Even if you are aware of what triggers them and have tried some steps to overcome the unpleasant feelings that come with them, outside support can be helpful. You might decide that you need this extra support to reinforce what you have already learned and practiced. Your first line of support may be your parents, school counselors, or members of the clergy. Or, you may want to start with your family physician. Then you could turn to professionals who are trained in helping people who have mental-health concerns. Your physician can help make an appropriate referral.

Seeking professional help is taking an important step in the right direction. Talking with a professional is a sign of strength. Doing so means that you are taking control of your situation. A counselor or therapist can make a

Talking with a professional is a sign of strength. Doing so means that you are taking control of your situation.

plan to help you conquer your phobia and will also provide an outlet for talking freely about your concerns.

What Is Counseling?

Counseling includes the professional services of psychologists, psychiatrists, social workers, and others. Counselors have completed training in their field and are usually certified by professional boards or state agencies. Your parents may want to help you look into their backgrounds before getting started.

Psychotherapy means talking about your emotional or mental concerns and working on the body, thought, and emotional reactions surrounding your fears. In psychotherapy,

Good Mental Health

Mental health involves a balance of mind, body, and spirit. Good mental health means that you can successfully perform mental tasks, get along well in school and with your friends, have satisfying relationships with other people, get involved in productive activities, and can adapt to change (such as working on overcoming phobias). With a good mental outlook, you have a sense of optimism in dealing with success as well as failure. You can expect to make some mistakes and still like yourself. You can view your disappointments in perspective, realizing that they are temporary and not permanent. With a healthy outlook, you understand that you don't have to generalize about life based on one unpleasant event.

you and your therapist will form a relationship to focus constructively on your symptoms. This relationship can help you get over patterns of unwanted behavior, such as fear reactions, compulsions, and low self-esteem. Psychotherapy does not involve taking medication, although in some cases, a combination of talking therapy and medication may be advised.

Alex used to be afraid to go to the doctor. "I felt faint and nauseated when I saw a needle or even thought about one. I was sick a lot when I was little and had to get shots. I used to really scream and didn't know why." When Alex turned eleven he wanted to go to summer camp, but certain shots were required. Although he wanted to go, he refused to get the shots—even though it meant he might not be able to attend camp. "My mom found a therapist who taught me how to relax and gradually got me used to the idea of having shots. So I had the shots and I had a good time at camp."

Alex's therapist used a technique known as exposure therapy. During the first few visits, they talked about his phobia of needles and how his body felt when he thought or talked about needles and shots. She showed him pictures of young people having shots. They talked about how he felt while looking at the pictures. Then she showed him a video of people getting shots in doctors' offices. She asked him to imagine having a shot himself and, at the same time, doing deep-breathing exercises and trying to relax. With gradual exposure, she finally showed him the needle that the doctor would use. He learned to relax while looking at it. Finally, Alex agreed to go to the doctor and get the necessary shot. He did the breathing exercise on the way to the doctor's office. His doctor understood Alex's fear and explained exactly what he would do. Alex got his shot and felt good about himself for working on his phobia.

People with phobias are often prevented from doing things they really want to do. Alex would not have gone to camp if he didn't face his needle phobia. You may also suffer from physical symptoms when you confront your fears— or even think about them. That's when a therapist can help.

Choosing a Therapist

Any therapist you choose will be on your side and will keep your discussions private. Some schools have social workers or counselors who can refer you to mental-health professionals who specialize in young people's anxieties and fears. If your school doesn't have anyone to make a referral, there may be a community mental-health center where you live. Its staff can help you find the best type of therapist for you.

There are several kinds of mental-health professionals. These include psychologists, psychiatrists, and social workers who may work individually or as group therapists or family therapists.

Type of Therapist	What's Involved
Psychologist	Talking therapy and behavior modification
Psychiatrist	Talking therapy; can prescribe medications
Social worker	Talking therapy
Group therapist	Meeting and talking with people your age
Family therapist	Talking with you and your parents

Types of Psychotherapists

Psychologists are nonmedical specialists who diagnose and treat mental-health concerns. In most states, psychologists have a Ph.D. (Doctor of Philosophy) degree in psychology. Some specialize in young people's concerns such as school and social anxieties. Generally, psychologists will work with your specific phobia and unwanted reactions or behaviors that cause you to seek help. They will be supportive and will help you plan ways to change your reactions and behaviors.

Psychologists may also help you change your reactions and behaviors with a technique called behavior modification. This form of therapy focuses on learned responses. Behavior therapists regard phobias as situations that have a learned component. They try to replace unwanted behaviors (such as fear reactions) with more desirable behaviors (such as being calm in the face of the scary situation). Behavior therapy has helped many young people who have social phobias—and other specific phobias—as well as obsessions and compulsions.

Cognitive Behavior Therapy

Cognitive therapy, like behavior therapy, can help a young person to recognize and change unwanted thoughts, attitudes, and behaviors, such as responses in feared situations. This technique emphasizes changing one's thoughts, feelings, and attitudes to change the unwanted behaviors.

Psychiatrists are medical doctors who diagnose and treat emotional concerns. They can prescribe medications and, when necessary, can admit people to hospitals. Most psychiatrists are trained in a variety of ways to diagnose and treat problems but many also use medication to help

Behavior therapists try to replace unwanted behaviors (such as fear reactions) with more desirable behaviors (such as being calm in the face of the scary situation).

people cope with fear and anxiety. A psychiatrist should cooperate with your family physician so that your total health care can be coordinated. This is important because if you are advised to take a medication by the psychiatrist, your physician will be sure that a new medication will not interfere with any other medications you are taking.

Social workers are trained in a wide variety of thera-pies to help people with phobias and other anxieties. Social workers can be helpful by getting to know you and understanding your problems. They listen and discuss your situation and may offer some practical suggestions to help you get better. When necessary, they can refer you to further sources for assistance, such as psychologists, psychiatrists, or family or group therapy.

Thirteen-year-old Becky found that *group therapy,* guided by a social worker, helped her resolve problems. "Looking at pictures in teen magazines, I was afraid that I was really fat," recalls Becky. "I always wore loose clothes, and became obsessed with getting really thin. Eventually, I nearly stopped eating, and I lost weight big-time."

Becky's parents noticed her problem, and they worked with Becky's family doctor to get her into a support group with other kids who were afraid of being fat. "Sharing feelings with the social worker and the other kids really helped. Now I like my body and eat healthy foods."

Becky was able to change her unhealthy and life-threatening habit of extreme weight loss (anorexia) by meeting with others like herself. Becky's group learned not to be afraid of food and to understand that food is necessary for good health. The counselor for the group, a social worker, slowly retrained them in how to think about themselves and how to eat. Group therapy can also be helpful for other phobias, such as social phobias, eating disorders, and obsessions and compulsions.

A *family therapist* may be necessary if your fears are shared by or are connected to your family life. This will involve you and one or more parents, guardians, or siblings. This kind of therapy is based on the idea that a troubled person should be considered part of a family unit. The counselor or therapist can encourage open communication so conflicts and disturbances involving family relationships can be discussed or changed. Family therapy usually focuses on practical solutions, such as parents reassuring the fearful child that locks on the house are burglar proof.

"Since I was little, my mother told me about her terrible experience in childbirth," says Vanessa. "She was afraid to go to doctors, and that made me afraid, too." Vanessa's fear of doctors was discovered when she fainted in gym class, and the school nurse found out that Vanessa hadn't had a checkup in a long time. Her mother took her to the doctor and Vanessa found out that she was anemic. "The doctor recommended that Mom and I go together for family counseling to help us get over our fear of doctors. I'm glad I did. Now I can play sports in gym and feel good."

"The doctor recommended that Mom and I go together for family counseling to help us get over our fear of doctors."

Therapists of many types help young people develop skills to identify fears as well as the sensations in their bodies, thoughts, and behavioral reactions attached to those fears. For example, young people who have social fears learn to identify and then change their worries that increase feelings of anxiety in social situations. By thinking positive thoughts, young people are better able to participate in and enjoy social situations.

Learning by Observation
One way therapists help young people overcome a phobia

is by modeling a preferred behavior in response to fear. In other words, by watching the therapist react to a scary situation in a calm and confident way, the young person can learn to follow the same behavior. Modeling is really learning by observation. Sometimes stories or videotapes are used. For example, for a young person afraid of water, a therapist might "model" going into a swimming pool by telling a story or showing a video. The physical and emotional reactions of the therapist would be positive and encouraging. With appropriate repetition and eventual exposure to water, the young person who has been fearful of water would be able to enter the water with confidence.

Using breathing and relaxation techniques as coping skills and tools, a young person can learn to face and overcome fears. Exposure to fearful situations and learning new ways to respond to those situations are important in the fear-reducing process. The ideas presented in this book may be the first place to start if your fears are moderate. If they are intense, use these tips and seek outside help. A counselor or therapist will know the best ways to help you. Because your phobia is unique to you, the therapist will plan a tailor-made program for you to overcome your phobia. Over time, you will be able to successfully face the situation, person, or thing that causes your phobia.

GLOSSARY

adolescence: the term for the period of life between when secondary sexual characteristics appear and when physical growth ceases; although different for each individual, adolescence generally encompasses pre-teen and early teen years

agoraphobia: a condition in which one has extreme anxiety about being in places or situations from which getting out might be embarrassing or difficult, or in which help may not be readily available

anger: an intense emotional state in which one feels a high level of displeasure, frustration, and stress

anxiety: an unpleasant feeling of generalized fear, often accompanied by tension in the body behavior modification: a type of therapy used by mental-health professionals that stresses the effect of learning on behavior; in this therapy, specific goals and desired new behaviors are outlined and progress is evaluated toward those goals

catastrophize: imagining that the worst-case scenario will happen; people who catastrophize sometimes have low self-esteem and may be shy in social situations

circle of fear: a fear of the body sensations that come along with reactions to fear; then the body sensations themselves trigger or cause the fear reaction

cognitive behavior therapy: a type of therapy to help one change unwanted behaviors, such as reactions to feared situations

coping: solutions one finds for anxiety-producing, as well as everyday, situations

exposure therapy: a type of behavior therapy aimed at changing an individual's fearful reactions and responses by gradually increasing his or her exposure to the phobic situation

family therapy: mental health counseling that focuses on practical solutions for the family unit to relate better to one another; family members become aware of how they deal with each other and are encouraged to communicate more openly with each other fear trigger: situations, things or people that make one start to feel afraid; it may be a sight, smell, sound, feeling, or thought that reminds one of a fearful situation

group therapy: treatment of emotional or psychological concerns in groups of people led by a mental health professional; such groups help people with similar concerns, such as those concerned with overweight or shyness

meditation: a technique to relieve stress, involving deep relaxation brought on by focused attention on a particular sound or image and breathing deeply

nausea: a common symptom of fear that is a feeling of sickness in one's stomach and a feeling of wanting to vomit

nervous: a feeling of tension, worry, and restlessness; a form of anxiety

obsessive-compulsive disorder: obsessions are persistent, intense, senseless, worrisome, and often revolting thoughts, ideas, or impulses that involuntarily come into one's mind; compulsions are repetitive and seemingly purposeful acts that result from these obsessions, in which the person does certain acts in a way to prevent or avoid imagined bad consequences phobia: an irrational, intense fear of a situation or sensation that is not shared by others and is out of proportion to the real danger; phobias can be of specific things, such as elevators, or of social situations (social phobia)

post-traumatic stress disorder (PTSD): this affects many young people after a major life trauma, such as a school shooting, local tragedy, automobile accident, or a national disaster; symptoms include repeated episodes of experiencing the traumatic event, which happens suddenly with vivid memories and painful emotional feelings

psychotherapy: talking about your emotional or mental health concerns with a trained mental health professional; psychotherapy is provided by psychologists, psychiatrists, and trained social workers

relaxation: a feeling of freedom from anxiety and worry

ritual: an unwanted activity that one repeats to reduce fear

self-esteem: the positive light in which one sees oneself; it is liking oneself and appreciating one's good qualities, and having confidence to conduct oneself successfully in various life situations shyness: a symptom of social anxiety, related to a fear of being unfavorably evaluated or criticized by others; the shy person may feel insecure and may have actual physical symptoms in certain situations, such as sweating or blushing

social phobia: a fear of being evaluated, criticized, or embarrassed in social settings; social phobias include fears of speaking, blushing, or being sick in front of others

social worker: a skilled professional, usually with a master's degree in social work, who carries out individual, family, and group psychotherapy

stage fright: a fear of speaking or performing in front of an audience; it involves a fear of making a mistake in front of others or looking foolish and affects people when they are being evaluated, such as making a speech or playing a musical instrument

trauma: a past experience that affects one's later life and one's ability to deal with fears and anxieties

worry: a feeling of uneasiness and mental discomfort about something that may occur in the future

FURTHER RESOURCES

Books

Giacobello, John. *Everything You Need to Know About Anxiety and Panic Attacks.* New York: The Rosen Publishing Group, 2000.

Lee, Jordan. *Coping with Anxiety and Panic Disorder.* New York: The Rosen Publishing Group, 1997.

Monroe, Judy. *Phobias: Everything You Wanted to Know, but Were Afraid to Ask.* Springfield, NJ: Enslow Publishers, 1996.

Tashjian, Janet. *Multiple Choice.* New York: Henry Holt, 1999.

Trueit, Trudi Strain. *Eating Disorders.* Danbury, CT: Franklin Watts, 2003.

Online Sites and Organizations

American Academy of Child and Adolescent Psychiatry
3615 Wisconsin Ave., NW
Washington, DC 20016
(202) 966-7300
www.aacap.org

American Group Psychotherapy Association
25 E. Twenty-first St., Sixth Floor
New York, NY 10010
(877) 668-2472, (212) 477-2677
www.agpa.org

American Psychiatric Association
1000 Wilson Blvd., Ste. 1825
Arlington, VA 22209
(888) 357-7924, (703) 907-7300
www.psych.org

American Psychological Association
750 First St., NE
Washington, DC 20002
(800) 374-2721, (202) 336-5500
www.apa.org

Anxiety Disorders Association of America
8730 Georgia Ave., Ste. 600
Silver Spring, MD 20910
(240) 485-1001
www.adaa.org

National Institute of Mental Health
6001 Executive Blvd., Rm. 8184, MSC 9663
Bethesda, MD 20892
(301) 443-4513
www.nimh.nih.gov

National Mental Health Association
2001 N. Beauregard St., Twelfth Floor
Alexandria, VA 22311
(800) 969-6642, (703) 684-7722
www.nmha.org

INDEX

ABOUT THE AUTHORS

Ada P. Kahn, Ph.D. is the author of *Stress A–Z: The Sourcebook for Coping with Everyday Challenges* and *Keeping the Beat: Healthy Aging Through Amateur Chamber Music Playing.* She has published more than forty articles on health-related subjects and worked as a health educator at a major hospital for more than ten years. She received her Ph.D. in public health from The Union Institute and University in Cincinnati, Ohio. She lives in Evanston, Illinois.

Ronald M. Doctor, Ph.D. is a first generation behavior therapist who is a licensed psychologist, a full professor at the California State University, Northridge, a researcher, author, and behavior-clinical practitioner. He is the author of more than forty journal articles and three books in the behavior modification areas, and a founding board member of the Anxiety Disorders Association of America. He received his Ph.D. from the University of Illinois in Champaign-Urbana. Ada P. Kahn, Ph.D. and Ronald M. Doctor, Ph.D. are co-authors of *Facing Fears: The Sourcebook for Everyday Phobias, Fears, and Anxieties* and *The Encyclopedia of Phobias, Fears, and Anxieties.*